Saving Se

Contents

written by Julie Suess

Sea turtles live in the ocean. Turtles have hard shells and big flippers for swimming.

These turtles can't pull their head and flippers inside their shells like other turtles. So they are easy to catch for hungry sharks.

Sea turtles must come up to the top of the water to get air. They come up every few minutes when they are swimming. They can hold their breath much longer when they rest and sleep.

There are 7 different kinds of sea turtles. They live in most oceans in the world.

The sea turtles are one of Earth's oldest animals. They are as old as the dinosaurs!

These sea turtles need our help. They have lived for millions of years, but now they are in danger.

People do lots of things that can hurt the sea turtles. Some people take them for their meat, eggs and shells. Turtles can get caught in fishing nets and drown.

9

Good people help keep the beaches clea
They pick up things that other people
have left on the beach. This stops bad
things from getting into the water.

10

Sea turtles think that plastic bags, balloons, and small pieces of plastic look like food. Turtles can get sick and die when they eat these things.

Mother turtles need a quiet and dark beach to lay their eggs. People help get the beach ready by making the sand flat.

nesting beach

eggs

People help to keep the eggs safe.
First, they watch the mother turtle as
she digs her nest and lays her eggs.

Next, they stop the eggs from being taken. When the baby turtles hatch, they watch them run safely to the sea.

People are working very hard to help save sea turtles in the water and on their nesting beaches.